CIVIL RIGHTS
THEN & NOW

A TIMELINE OF THE FIGHT FOR EQUALITY IN AMERICA

WRITTEN BY KRISTINA BROOKE DANIELE   DRAWINGS BY LINDSEY BAILEY

Woo! Jr. Kids Activities & Wendybird Press Founder: Wendy Piersall
Junior Art Director: Lilia Garvin
Cover Illustration: Michael Koch | Sleeping Troll Studios www.sleepingtroll.com
Interior Drawings: Lindsey Bailey | LindseySwop www.lindseyswop.com
Editing & Proofreading: Pam Sourelis & Lisa Messinger

Published by:
Wendybird Press
226 W. Judd
Woodstock IL, 60098
www.wendybirdpress.com

ISBN-13: 978-0997799354
ISBN-10: 0997799358

Contents

Dedication

For my mother, Martha Kennedy, who fed my reading habit
from an early age.

For Mr. Barnes, my middle school history teacher, who
challenged me to be better and to want more.

And especially for my daughter, Mya.
Never stop learning.
Never settle.
Never stop fighting.

The journey to this book began in August 1989. Although I did not know it then, this was a pivotal year in my understanding of the world as I started to spend more time with those who did not understand or embrace Blackness. In fact, the intersection of Black and White America was very limited, and usually came as the result of efforts on the part of those who looked like me.

Let me explain. I grew up on the corner of Morrison and Story Avenue in the Bronx, one of the five boroughs of New York City, in an apartment complex called Lafayette-Morrison. The four buildings were an anomaly in this area as they were not public housing. Rent was determined by income, and most tenants were either working class or middle class. Although safer than many Bronx neighborhoods, Lafayette-Morrison was an "island" surrounded on four sides by some pretty tough ones!

When I played outside with friends, it was usually in my neighborhood in a shared grassy area between the buildings known as the Circle. It's where I learned to ride a bike, roller skate, play manhunt, dribble a basketball, and jump double Dutch with children who mostly looked like me. But, while my neighborhood was predominately Black and Latinx, my sisters and I rode public transportation to Manhattan where we took ballet, tap, African dance, and piano lessons at Harlem School of the Arts. Tap and African dance were taught by teachers who looked like me, and my piano, voice, and ballet were taught by White teachers.

During the summers, my sisters and I went to sleepaway camp, first at Clear Pool in Carmel, New York, then at Minisink in Dover Plains, and even with The Fresh Air Fund, an organization that offered inner-city children a taste of country living in Upstate New York.

Most of the counselors were White, though most of the campers were not. One of the first years I attended, a White counselor stared at my tightly coiled, coarse hair with confusion right before she cut it all off because she did not know how to manage it. She was lost in dealing with something that was my standard.

My sisters and I did not attend the public schools in our neighborhood. When we weren't being taught at home, we went to PS 14 and IS 192 in Throggs Neck, a mostly White area of the Bronx. While the students at these schools were predominantly White, there were enough Black and Latinx children to provide some comfort. Yet none of my teachers were Black. And in the gifted classes in which I was placed, very few of the students looked like me.

A month before the 1989 school year began, my mom withdrew me from public school and enrolled me in private school. We visited several private schools, including Horace Mann and Riverdale, two elite college prep schools in the Bronx, although they did their best to hide that their large campuses were part of the borough. As we walked through their halls, eyes stared at us with wonder. We chose Columbia Grammar and Preparatory School, a small college prep school located in three brownstone buildings on Central Park West in Upper Manhattan because that area of the city was more diverse.

The truth of economic disparity experienced during my daily commute was hard to ignore. My bus rolled through neighborhoods that my mom warned me to stay away from and into the most exclusive areas. Billboards for cigarettes and liquor turned into advertisements for Broadway theater and high fashion. In school, our lunches were catered and consisted of fresh vegetables as opposed to the hardly edible, public school cafeteria lunches. We were given beautiful novels and textbooks with bright pictures and no torn pages or scribblings, and sometimes we were given two copies of heavy books so that we didn't have to carry them home. There were no more than fifteen students in a subject class, and teachers knew us all by name.

I was the new kid from the Bronx struggling with imposter syndrome. As one of only six Black students in our grade, I felt more displaced than ever before. Maybe it was the numerous times that the Black students were asked to show ID to the front desk attendants when we entered the building because they were sure we didn't belong there. Or maybe it was that my White English teacher believed that I wrote the lyrics to the rap song, "A Children's Story" by Slick Rick. It could also have been the divide between the high school's large Jewish population and its small Black and Latinx population, which stemmed from a lack of knowledge and the discomfort that talking about racism brings.

Whatever it was, as I look back now I realize that my childhood was spent adapting to and reshaping myself to fit in White spaces. I fought for a voice that wasn't stifled by the trappings of stereotypes and racial bias. It is rare that Black, Indigenous, or people of color can go our entire lives without interacting with a White person, so there is no chance for us to avoid the discomfort of racism. Yet White people can go their whole lives without ever interacting with a Black person. In fact, many do, and most will never know what it is like to form their own identity in a world that tells them that they are not good enough. Or normal. Or accepted.

In our current political climate, it is easy to lose sight of the truth. It is not difficult to fall victim to "alternative facts" spouted by those who choose willful ignorance. What is difficult is *change*. I hope that this book, although condensed for time and understanding, will help you acknowledge this struggle for freedom. I hope it also opens your eyes to how many of the civil rights that we are fighting for today are the same civil rights that others fought for in the 1950s and 1960s.

How should you use this book?

- If you are a parent or teacher, please read it through first.

- If something presented in *Civil Rights: Then and Now* makes you uncomfortable, ask yourself why. Together we can confront any misunderstandings and preconceived notions.

- Take this book slowly! It's not too long, but it is packed with information. Discuss the things presented here with your children.

- Read the authentic experiences of marginalized people by using the *Suggested Reading List* on page 73 to find books written from another perspective.

The last time I checked, progress was also a verb, so don't stop pushing forward!

- Kristina Brooke Daniele

A Brief Overview
of the American Civil Rights Movement

The term *civil rights* refers to the freedom of citizens to live equally in society. The American Civil Rights Movement of the 1950s and 1960s refers to the combined efforts of people throughout the United States who organized protests, voter registration drives, and other community events with the purpose of ending legal discrimination against Black people. While often peaceful, many of these efforts turned violent due to harsh retaliation by government agents, police, and White people who wanted to preserve the status quo by keeping intact segregation and systemic racism.

Systemic, or institutional, racism is an established system of laws, policies, and practices that deprive one group of resources while protecting and providing those resources for the group in power. Civil disobedience, or acts of peaceful rebellion against unjust laws, in which citizens engaged to dismantle systemic racism and inequality, was one of the most effective methods of resistance at this time.

The Civil Rights Movement specifically addressed the race and skin-color based laws that were designed to discriminate and separate. Since the practices that infringed upon the rights of Black Americans were legal, the American Civil Rights Movement sought to overturn these laws and give Black Americans the same inalienable rights as White Americans.

Civil rights for Black people in the United States has been an issue of debate since our founders declared independence from Great Britain in 1776.

Slavery, the practice in which one group of human beings is owned as property and forced into servitude by another, has long divided the country. Because enslaved people were considered chattel, or property, many White people believed Black people were not entitled to the same rights that they held, and therefore accepted the institution of slavery. This argument was dependent on the unfounded bias of skin color that stemmed from the Judeo-Christian misinterpretation of the Curse of Canaan, also known as the Curse of Ham. The story goes that Ham, the father of the Canaan people, witnessed his father Noah's drunkenness and did not look away. In anger, Noah cursed Ham to a life of servitude. Clearly, the issue of slavery was one in which religion and politics were dangerously intertwined, despite America being founded as a place of religious freedom and decreed by our founders to be a country in which the government would remain untainted by religion. The legal practice of slavery divided the country and continued to do so despite being abolished by the 13th Amendment.

Deeply held religious beliefs, coupled with politics, can create quite a divide. When Thomas Jefferson, who himself was a slave owner, wrote early drafts of the Declaration of Independence, he spoke out against the horrors of the slave trade, but not against slavery itself. However, the Continental Congress chose not to include any mention of slavery or the slave trade in the final draft of the document, as they believed that,

The Emancipation Proclamation, *signed by President Abraham Lincoln in 1863, ordered the release of slaves in the 10 rebelling southern states. Slavery would not be fully abolished until 1865.*

because African people were bought and sold, they were personal property and the government could not tell its citizens what to do with their property.

Both the British and the Colonists' Armies recruited escaped and enslaved African men to fight in the American Revolution. It was common practice to promise them freedom, which they would receive when the war was won. Most enslaved people who fought did not, in fact, receive their freedom, and the fight to abolish slavery continued.

In fact, some of the earliest civil rights leaders were abolitionists who were active in the fight against slavery.

Of course, abolishing slavery was just the beginning of the fight for civil rights. Once Congress ratified the 13th Amendment in 1865, as well as the 14th Amendment in 1868, Black people were granted citizenship as natural-born Americans. On paper, this meant that they now had all the rights given to White people, and Black men now had the right to vote. Yet it would take more than a hundred years for the federal government to uphold the rights that they had given on paper to people of color.

*Many public spaces such as restrooms remained segregated for an entire **century** after slavery was abolished.*

Frederick Douglass 1818-1895

Douglass, who escaped slavery, became one of the leading abolitionists of his time. His autobiography, which he revised and republished three times, made him extremely popular but also made him the target of recapture attempts. He traveled the world speaking about the evils of slavery and worked with Elizabeth Stanton to promote women's suffrage. He was also the first Black American nominated for Vice President of the United States.

Harriet Tubman 1822-1913

An enslaved woman who escaped captivity and went on to lead the Underground Railroad. She helped to free 700 enslaved people and served as the first woman to lead an armed expedition during the Civil War.

Important
Abolitionists & Activists

Booker T. Washington 1856-1915

An enslaved man who was emancipated, Booker T. Washington became one of the most influential leaders of Black liberation. He believed that former slaves should focus more on vocational studies and community building, and less on attempts to fight segregation. He became the first president of Tuskegee University and helped to form the National Negro League. In 1895, Booker T. Washington and other Black leaders struck a deal with southern White leaders. This agreement was never written down or formally recorded. In it, Booker T. Washington and others agreed that Black people in the South would submit to segregation, not ask for the right to vote, nor retaliate against racial violence or try to end discrimination. In return, they would receive a free basic vocational education (mechanics, teaching, nursing, etc.). W. E. B. Du Bois named it the Atlanta Compromise.

W.E.B. Du Bois 1868-1963

A social justice activist, Du Bois helped found the NAACP. He was the first Black American to receive a Ph.D. from Harvard University. Du Bois fought against racism and discrimination in education and employment. He actively spoke out against lynching and Jim Crow laws. He also fought against the idea of the genetic superiority of the White race, writing numerous dissenting essays and articles. His collection of essays _The Souls of Black Folks_ serves as an example of the great intellect and humanity of Black people. Although he believed in equality for all, he did not speak out in favor of women's voting rights because the leaders of the Woman Suffrage Movement did not actively and publicly support Black rights. Du Bois was against the Atlanta Compromise, believing that Black people should fight for equality and rights.

Nat Turner 1800-1831

Born into slavery, Nat Turner led one of the bloodiest revolts against slavery in the United States. He believed that he was chosen by God to fight evil. He led a group of 50 slaves who traveled to different plantations and killed White slave owners, women, and children. His rebellion caused harsher laws against southern abolitionists but also garnered the support of northerners who believed that slavery was wrong.

The South After the Civil War
(Reconstruction)

Jim Crow laws, named for a minstrel routine that degraded Black Americans, consisted of any legislation that served to keep segregation intact. These laws, many passed in 1870, required that Blacks and Whites remain separated on public transportation, in parks, cemeteries, schools, and theaters. There were separate water fountains, and Black people were often forced to enter buildings through the back door, also known as the servants' entrance. Additionally, there were laws that made interracial marriage illegal. The goal was to prevent interaction between races and to continue the notion that the races were not equal.

The fight for civil rights came front and center on a broader scale in 1955 when Rosa Parks, a Black woman employed as a secretary at the **National Association for the Advancement of Colored People (NAACP)**, refused to give up her seat in the front row of the "Colored Only" section to a White man on a Montgomery, Alabama bus. She was arrested for failing to adhere to the city's segregation laws. Sitting was not her first act of protest against this very issue, nor was Parks the first person to protest in this way. Yet her decision to no longer accept the humiliation of segregation laws sparked the Montgomery Bus Boycott, with Dr. Martin Luther King Jr. as its spokesperson. Although Rosa Park's arrest was the catalyst for the boycott, its roots can be traced back to a letter written

by **The Women's Political Council (WPC)**, a group of Black women who were civil rights activists and who were already planning a boycott of the Montgomery bus system.

———— •◆• ————

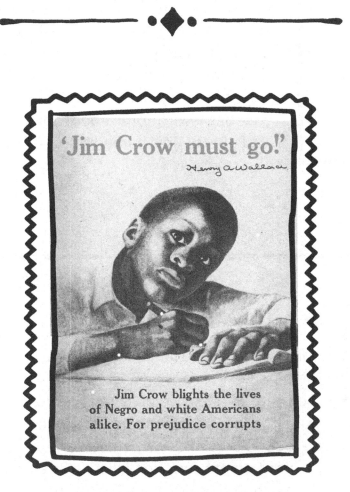

This newspaper clipping was printed in 1948 during Henry Wallace's failed presidential campaign. Henry Wallace served as Vice President from 1941-1945.

The purpose of the Montgomery Bus Boycott was not to repeal segregation laws, but rather to force the city to hire more Black bus drivers. Its organizers also sought to change the seating policy to one that allowed seats to be filled on a first-come-first-served basis, and to demand to be treated with respect and courtesy. The boycott included 40,000 riders who refused to ride the buses for 381 days. But despite the success of the boycott, it wasn't until Aurelia Browder, Susie McDonald, Claudette Colvin, and Mary Louise Smith brought a civil lawsuit against the bus company that the boycott elicited positive change. Their case, **Browder v Gayle** (1956) was used by the Supreme Court to end segregation on buses. The Supreme Court's ruling increased the momentum of the American Civil Rights Movement.

" People always say that I didn't give up my seat because I was tired, but that isn't true. I was not tired physically... No, the only tired I was, was tired of giving in. "

Rosa Parks

It was not the first time that the Supreme Court had shot down state-sponsored segregation. The ruling in the case, **Brown v Board of Education of Topeka** (1954), which was argued by NAACP attorney Thurgood Marshall, had overturned segregation and declared that "separate but equal schools were inherently unequal." This decision struck down the ruling in **Plessy v Ferguson** (1896), which stated that if the facilities and services offered to Black Americans were equal to those offered to White Americans, segregation was legal. However, since many White people believed Black people were inferior, local governments often ignored the "equal" portion of Plessy's "separate but equal" ruling. The ruling in **Brown v Board of Education** forced states to integrate their public schools. Between this ruling and that of **Browder v Gayle**, desegregation was underway.

Dr. Martin Luther King Jr.'s unique ability to inspire the public with his speeches made him the face of the movement. His use of non-violent protests, which publicly shamed the very violent police and government officials who tried to suppress the movement, made him hugely popular among Christians. To that end, he was elected president of the newly-formed **Southern Christian Leadership Conference** (SCLC), where he continued to lead and preach about the power of love in moving the nation forward. However, much of the progress made by the movement was due to lesser-known activists and organizations.

" Injustice anywhere is a threat to justice everywhere. "

Martin Luther King Jr.
Letter from the Birmingham Jail

In Summary...

The most notable accomplishments of the Civil Rights Movement of these two decades were those that established Black people as equal citizens and paved the way to help other marginalized groups gain equality. As mentioned previously, the Supreme Court decisions that deemed segregation a violation of human rights contributed to pushing the movement toward a unified society. "Separate but equal" was overturned and schools were integrated. President Lyndon Johnson and Congress passed the **Voting Rights Act of 1965**, which increased the number of Black Americans registered to vote by making illegal the policies that created barriers to voting.

However, systemic racism has not been dismantled. It has continued to erode the fabric of American unity. Not only are Black people fighting against attempts to revert the country to the Jim Crow era, many of the protections for women, the disabled, the poor, the Lesbian, Gay, Bisexual, Transgender, and Queer, or Questioning (**LGBTQ**) community, and immigrants are also at risk, leaving these marginalized groups to fear for their well-being and their rights. The Civil Rights Movement has evolved to meet these new challenges, and are discussed in part 2.

Civil Rights Era
Movements & Leaders

The Women's Political Council

The Women's Political Council galvanized a generation of protestors, providing a framework for peaceful protest nationwide.

Started by Mary Fair Burks and made of mostly middle class, educated, Black professionals, the **Women's Political Council (WPC)** aspired to encourage Black Americans to aim for success and to rise above mediocrity. They focused on encouraging political and civic involvement through lobbying and increasing voter registration. While Dr. Martin Luther King Jr. is the most well-known figure of the Montgomery Bus Boycott, the WPC was the organizing force behind the protest. The WPC was largely responsible for motivating middle class Black Americans to become involved in the fight for civil rights.

Emmett Till

Fourteen-year-old Emmett Till traveled from Chicago to Money, Mississippi, to visit family in 1955. After purchasing candy at a White-owned store, he was accused of touching, whistling at, and making lewd comments to the store owner's wife, Carolyn Bryant. Three days later, he was abducted from his uncle's home by Ray Bryant and Ray's half-brother, who tortured and brutally murdered him. His attackers never denied their involvement, yet a jury of their peers found them not guilty.

His mother ensured that his body was visible by insisting that the casket remain open during his funeral, which was held in Chicago. *Jet* magazine published photos of his brutalized body, which helped to mobilize northerners to join the fight for civil rights. In 2017, the woman who accused Emmett Till and ultimately caused his murder admitted to making up the story and lying to the FBI about the incident. She was not charged with obstruction of justice, as the five-year statute of limitations had run out.

> God told me, "I have taken one from you, but I will give you thousands."

Mamie Till-Mobley
Mother of Emmett Till

New York City Mayor Robert Wagner Jr. greeted the Little Rock Nine in 1958.

Little Rock Nine
1957

Nine Black students, known as the "Little Rock Nine", became the first students to integrate Little Rock Central High School in Arkansas. President Dwight D. Eisenhower had to intervene for their protection, as the mayor of Little Rock blocked their entry into the school.

Ruby Bridges
1960

The first Black child to integrate William Frantz Elementary School in New Orleans was a six-year-old girl. She endured boycotts, ridicule, and death threats, and she and her mother had to be escorted by federal marshals during her first year at the school. Due to threats of poisoning, she was not allowed to eat food that she did not bring to school herself.

" Kids know nothing about racism. They're taught that by adults. "

Ruby Bridges

Sit-Ins

—————◆—————

"Those students from Lane who were doing the sit-ins, they were the most disciplined young people I've ever seen in my life."

John Parish
Jackson Sun Reporter

The most famous sit-in took place on February 1, 1960, at a Woolworth's department store lunch counter. It is often regarded by many as the start of the Civil Rights Movement. Franklin McCain, David Richmond, Joseph McNeil, and Ezell Blair, Black students at North Carolina A&T University sat at the whites-only counter and asked to be served. Their request was denied but the young men remained seated, waiting for their coffee.

Student Non-Violent Coordinating Committee

A student organization formed from a meeting headed by Ella Baker, a young student activist at Shaw University. The members travelled across the South during what was called Freedom Summer, helping to register Black people to vote. Their goal was political activity and awareness. Stokley Carmichael, who assumed leadership, worked to shift the focus of the organization to protesting the Vietnam War and to promoting Black Power - the celebration and redefining of Black history and pride. Unsure that they could continue their non-violent actions due to increased violence from the public and police, the organization changed its name to **Student National Coordinating Committee (SNCC)**.

Fannie Lou Hamer

A civil rights activist who, after being beaten by police while held on false charges, returned to Mississippi to focus on registering Black Americans to vote so that they could leverage their political power. She was also a member of the SNCC and helped to organize their Freedom Rides across the South in support of sit-ins and other acts of resistance. The mixed-race groups of students traveled on buses, sitting together in opposition of the still-segregated buses that were deemed illegal by the Supreme Court.

Hamer was also Vice Chair of the Mississippi Freedom Democratic Party. In 1964, she ran for Congress, but lost. After her loss, she worked to implement several Head Start programs and then turned her attention to helping Black people gain freedom and equality through land ownership.

"If I fall, I'll fall five feet four inches forward in the fight for freedom. I'm not backing off."
Fannie Lou Hamer

The Black Panther Party for Self Defense

Founded in 1966 by Huey P. Newton and Bobby Seale, the **Black Panther Party** was labeled a militant organization by the head of the FBI, J. Edgar Hoover. In truth, the Black Panther Party was a community organization that encouraged Black Americans to know their rights when dealing with police officers, and to learn to use firearms to protect themselves and their communities. They did not promote the use of violence but felt that when violence was used against them, Black Americans should fight back.

Chapters of the Black Panther Party sprung up all over the United States. The Black Panther Party for Self Defense started The Free Breakfast Program in Oakland, California. Its success encouraged others to begin free breakfast programs and Head Start programs at inner-city schools and churches throughout the United States, many with the help of The Party. The Party's Ten-Point Program called for better education and jobs for Black people, an end to unjust treatment and practices, and fair trials that included Black people on juries.

Malcolm X

Born Malcolm Little, Malcolm X changed his name after converting to Islam. He became prominent in the Civil Rights Movement, offering an alternative to Dr. Martin Luther King Jr's non-violent stance. Malcolm X urged members of the Black community to organize, know their rights, and be ready to fight for justice. He thought that violent resistance was a useful option and could help secure freedom for the oppressed.

However, after breaking with the Nation of Islam and completing a pilgrimage to Mecca, he returned to the United States more optimistic about non-violent revolution. Malcolm X began to embrace what he called "sincere" White allies and preach about the unification of Black and brown peoples. He firmly believed that White people had an obligation to teach each other about the evils of racism, but he believed that this would only happen at the behest of Black people. He was assassinated on February 21, 1965.

Landmark
Cases & Amendments

from Slavery through the 1960s

An addition to the United States Constitution that officially abolished slavery.

14th Amendment
July 9, 1868

United States v. Stanley
1883

13th Amendment
December 6, 1865

An addition to the United States Constitution that addresses citizenship rights and equal protection of the laws to all natural born citizens.

Neither the 13th nor the 14th Amendment empowers Congress to safeguard Blacks against the actions of private individuals. To have decided otherwise would have afforded Blacks a special status under the law that Whites did not enjoy.

The Court overturned the convictions of the "Scottsboro boys," nine Black men who were wrongfully convicted of raping a White woman on a freight train in Scottsboro, Alabama, stating that the right to an attorney was essential to a fair trial.

The Court ruled that the "separate but equal" provision of private services mandated by state government is constitutional under the Equal Protection Clause. *(See vocabulary list.)*

Meyer v. Nebraska
1923

Plessy v. Ferguson
1896

Powell v. Alabama
1932

The Court ruled that a 1919 Nebraska law prohibiting the teaching of modern foreign languages to grade-school children violated the Due Process Clause of the 14th Amendment.

Yick Wo v. Hopkins
1886

This is the first time the Supreme Court ruled that when a law, which as written does not specifically discriminate against any one group, is applied in a way that is racially discriminatory, it violates the Equal Protection Clause of the 14th Amendment.

The Court ruled that "separate educational facilities are inherently unequal," thus striking down **Plessy v. Ferguson** (1896).

The Court ruled that prohibiting the ownership of property based on race is a violation of the Equal Protection Clause of the 14th Amendment.

This was the first Mexican-American civil rights case to make it to the Supreme Court. The Court ruled that Mexican Americans and all other racial and national groups in the United States had equal protection under the 14th Amendment to the U.S. Constitution.

Brown v. Board of Education
1954

Shelley v. Kraemer
1948

Hernandez v. Texas
1954

Did you **Know**?

*Both **Brown v. Board of Education** and **Hernandez v. Texas** received unanimous rulings by the Warren Supreme Court, pictured left, which means all nine Supreme Court Justices ruled the same way.*

Landmark Cases & Amendments

> " Gideon did write that letter, the Court did look into his case ... and the whole course of American legal history has been changed. "
>
> **Robert F. Kennedy**
> Attorney General

The Court held that school systems must abolish their racially dual systems (separate but equal), but that each jurisdiction had different issues and therefore could do so in their own time.

The Court ruled that the 6th Amendment right to counsel is a fundamental right and must be applied to the states via the 14th Amendment's Due Process Clause. It requires that criminal defendants of impoverished means be provided counsel at trial.

Brown v. Board II
1955

Browder v. Gayle
1956

Gideon v. Wainwright
1963

The Court upheld the lower court ruling that the segregation of public buses was unconstitutional.

The Court upheld that Congress could force private businesses to uphold the **Civil Rights Act of 1964** based on the Interstate Commerce Clause of the U.S. Constitution. If the business provides services to customers traveling between states, it must adhere to federal law.

The Court ruled that state laws that prohibited interracial marriage were unconstitutional and held that marriage was a fundamental right.

The Court extended the 6th Amendment right to counsel rule to apply even during police interrogation and specifically stating that government or police cannot bypass a defendant's lawyer to speak directly to the defendant.

Massiah v. United States & Miranda v. Arizona
1964 & 1966

Loving v. Virginia
1967

Heart of Atlanta Motel Inc v. United States & Katzenbach v. McClung
1964

Questions for Comprehension

Multiple Choice

1. Which of the following are considered civil rights? (Circle all that apply.)

   A. Voting and protesting unjust laws
   B. Refusing service to someone based on skin color
   C. Marrying whomever you love
   D. Going to school

2. Which of these are NOT examples of systemic racism? (Circle all that apply.)

   A. School curricula that includes only the contributions of White Americans
   B. Scholarships for Hispanic students
   C. All-White juries
   D. Requiring employers and educational institutions to hire and accept a certain number of marginalized peoples

3. Who was responsible for the organization of the Montgomery Bus Boycott?

   A. Rosa Parks
   B. Martin Luther King Jr.
   C. The Women's Political Council
   D. The Black Panther Party for Self-Defense

4. Which of the following organizations were active in the Civil Rights Movement of the 1950s and 1960s? (Circle all that apply.)

   A. SNCC
   B. Black Lives Matter
   C. Occupy Wall Street
   D. The NAACP

True or False

5. _____ Those who fought against the practice of slavery were called abolitionists.

6. _____ The founders included slavery in the Declaration of Independence.

7. _____ Malcolm X and Dr. Martin Luther King Jr. both believed that non-violence was the only path to revolution.

8. _____ The Civil Rights Movement accomplished the desegregation of public places and schools.

Fill in the Blanks

9. The ruling in **Brown v Board of Education** forced states to _____ their public schools.

10. _____ was the first Black student to attend William Frantz Elementary School in New Orleans.

11. Many White people believed that they were _____ to Black people based on nothing more than their skin color.

12. Derived from a _____ act, Jim Crow laws aimed to prevent the mixing of races.

Short Answer Questions

13. Can one person own another person? Discuss and research "autonomy" and how that relates to the issue of slavery.

14. What are some examples of civil disobedience that you may have seen in your life? How does it make you feel? Do you agree or disagree with the act?

15. Have you heard stereotypes about other races or cultures? Discuss them in relation to reality. In what ways do stereotypes differ from reality?

16. Desegregating public spaces, especially schools, was very important at this time. Why?

17. What other civil rights activists from this time period have you heard of before? Share what you know about them.

18. Are there issues during the Civil Rights Movement of the 1950s and 1960s that are similar to some that are be addressed?

19. Why do you think racism is difficult for many people to discuss? What do you think about race, and how it relates to society?

20. In what ways did the Civil Rights Movement of the 1950s and 1960s help change things for all people of color?

Answers found on Page 70

The Modern American
Civil Rights Movement

The Current Fight for Civil Rights

The American Civil Rights Movement of the 1950s and the 1960s made significant advancements, yet the fight for civil rights is an ongoing battle. People of color still suffer greatly under systemic subjugation and the increasingly oppressive practices of government institutions. In the years that followed the Civil Rights Movement of the 1950s and 1960s, complacency has also plagued mainstream America because it is comprised of those who are seldom affected by discrimination and inequality. For marginalized groups, the fight continues.

Unfortunately, it has become increasingly difficult to fight against less visible signs of racism. During the Jim Crow era, laws were recognizably discriminatory and provided clear goals against which to rally. In the three decades since, the post-civil rights era has been fraught with covert suppression of rights, and the effects of systemic racism have been harder to bring to light. Moreover, with the election of President Ronald Reagan, the government began to focus more on corporate freedom and less on racial discrimination. His policies benefited corporations and the wealthiest U.S. citizens, and the growing opposition to civil rights was allowed to flourish. During his presidency, more than one million Americans experienced homelessness, and Reagan also closed many government agencies, including the Office of Domestic Violence. In fact, he vetoed the **Civil Rights Restoration Act of 1987**. Although Congress passed the bill, his actions sent a clear message to marginalized communities that there was a need for a new wave of civil rights advocacy.

The modern Civil Rights Movement has shifted toward a broader fight for human rights. The primary focus has centered on poverty, racism, police brutality, health care access, women's reproductive rights, marriage equality, and education.

> **❝ Penalties against possession of a drug should not be more damaging to an individual than the use of the drug itself. ❞**
>
> ## Jimmy Carter
> 39th U.S. President

Poverty and the War on Drugs

— •◆• —

In 1971, President Richard Nixon declared drugs to be "public enemy number one" and initiated a war on the sale and importation of drugs. Initially, all monies allocated to the War on Drugs went toward treatment rather than enforcement. The goal was to reduce the public's use and dependency on illegal drugs. However, by the 1980s, President Ronald Reagan had turned the focus to law enforcement and the criminalization of drug users. For over 40 years, law enforcement has disproportionately targeted Black, Latino, and Hispanic youth. Varying penalties imposed for variants of the same drug, cocaine, is an example of this bias. The powdered version, used mostly by White men, incurred significantly less punishment than the punishment for crack cocaine, a cheaper version predominantly used by Blacks, Indigenous, and People of Color (BIPOC). These non-White defendants also faced longer sentencing, and by the year 2000, one out of every three Black men in his twenties was in the criminal justice system. These young men were being deprived of educational opportunities, voting rights, employment, and housing opportunities. Treating drug users as criminals, rather than people in need of medical treatment, created a permanent social underclass.

The HIV & AIDS Epidemic

In 1981, the American public began to hear the first reports of what would be named Human Immunodeficiency Virus (HIV) and Acquired Immune Deficiency Syndrome (AIDS). Because most of those who showed signs of infection during the 1980s were intravenous drug users and members of the LGBTQ population, those who became infected were increasingly stigmatized. Many lost their jobs, were denied treatment in some hospitals, shunned by their religious and social communities, and even refused mortuary and funeral services upon their deaths. Additionally, because young people and members of racial and ethnic minority groups were disproportionately affected by HIV/AIDS, they were often the most economically impacted due to a lack of access to health care, educational resources, and birth control. Ongoing discrimination against those diagnosed with HIV/AIDS and the continued reduction of health care services to the disenfranchised has made it difficult for those living with the disease to find economic stability.

The Recessions of 1980 & 1982

These recessions were caused by the federal government raising interest rates to combat inflation. The economic downfall was further exacerbated by the Iranian oil embargo, which reduced U.S. oil reserves. Because of the limited supply, prices rose. Both businesses and citizens stopped spending money. Unemployment rose to 10.8 percent, the highest since 1933, and companies began laying off employees to save money. President Reagan partially ended the recession by lowering the tax rate and increasing the defense budget. Unfortunately, the unemployment rate remained high and never reached the lower levels of the pre-recession period. By the end of the recession, 92 banks had failed and 540 were in trouble. Unemployment had reached 11 percent. Manufacturing suffered considerably, as did construction and the automobile industry. Areas that relied heavily on factory employment were hit the hardest and not only struggled to recover, but to this day still haven't fully recovered.

" Our lives begin to end the day we become silent about the things that matter. *"*

Martin Luther King Jr.

Civil Liberties Act of 1988

This act, signed into law by President Ronald Reagan, issued a Presidential apology and issued a payment of $20,000 to those of Japanese ancestry who lost their freedom or property due to the discriminatory actions of the United States government after the 1941 bombing of Pearl Harbor. **Executive Order 9066**, issued in 1942 by Franklin D. Roosevelt, prohibited people of Japanese ancestry from living on the west coast of the United States, despite no proof of individual wrongdoing. Many were forced to leave their homes in California, Oregon, Washington, and Arizona, and were taken by the military to internment camps, where they were forced to live in captivity.

While this apology acknowledged the U.S. government's racism and discrimination against Asian-Americans, a formal apology for slavery and Jim Crow laws did not come until the U.S. House of Representatives issued a resolution in 2008.

> " Yet we must recognize that the internment of Japanese-Americans was just that: a mistake. For throughout the war, Japanese-Americans in the tens of thousands remained utterly loyal to the United States. "
>
> **Ronald Reagan**
> 40th U.S. President

Violent Crime Control and Law Enforcement Act of 1994

—◆—

President Bill Clinton later expressed regret over the portions of the Violent Crime Control and Law Enforcement Act that led to an increased prison population.

Written initially by then-Senator of Delaware, Joe Biden, **The Violent Crime Control and Law Enforcement Act** is one of the most controversial bills signed into law by President Bill Clinton. It was written in response to several instances of high-profile violent crimes, and President Clinton argued that it would reduce the number of Black Americans being killed in drug-related crimes. There were five significant facets to the act:

1. It allotted over $9.5 billion for the building of new federal prisons. These funds would be given to states if they agreed to create mandatory minimum sentences for crimes and if those convicted of violent crimes were forced to serve at least 85 percent of their prison sentence. This would drastically reduce the number of people released on early parole.
2. Inmates would no longer be provided Pell education grants to further their education.
3. It provided funding to help aid in the hiring of more than 100,000 new police officers throughout the country in order to put more officers on the street.
4. It created the "Three Strikes" rule, which required a mandatory life sentence for those convicted of three violent felonies.
5. It banned the manufacture of almost twenty semi-automatic firearms.

So why was this bill controversial? There were many reasons. The terminology that many politicians used to garner support for the bill painted Black children, who were engaging in behavior seemingly no different from their White peers, as "superpredators," a term used by Hillary Clinton to refer to urban gangs. As with the War on Drugs, much of the money allocated to fighting crime went to policing and incarceration rather than to prevention and rehabilitation. Bill Clinton's crime bill also helped to create a militarized police force that has become almost standard.

The United States also has one of the highest incarceration rates in the world, and this act increased the number of citizens arrested and imprisoned by offering states incentives for doing so. Moreover, due to the racially-charged methods of policing, many of those who suffered under this act were Black. While targeting Black people for incarceration has been a historical trend since the Reconstruction Era of Post-Civil War America, many believed that the 1994 crime act was a government-sanctioned attack against people of color.

The introduction of "Three Strikes" further indicated that rehabilitation was not the goal of incarceration and that recidivism was more desirable and more lucrative for state prisons. The law introduced almost seventy new felony offenses, as if to make it easier to charge people with crimes. Accused people are now forced to take plea-bargains even if they are innocent, for fear of being found guilty and sentenced to mandatory lengthy sentences.

Illegal Immigration Reform and Immigration Responsibility Act of 1996

Designed to improve border control, the **Illegal Immigration Reform and Immigration Responsibility Act** created and imposed severe penalties for creating fraudulent immigration documents and helping people illegally enter the United States. Undocumented immigrants who were accused of crimes were not allowed trials, and even legal immigrants faced deportation if convicted. It also made it more complicated for those who tried to gain legal status.

An individual who faced deportation would now have to prove that their deportation would cause a spouse, child, or someone else, to suffer an unusual hardship. Even the separation of a family was not enough to allow a person to remain in the United States. Additionally, only three thousand immigrants per year would be allowed this exception. Another facet of this law prevented immigrants from directly applying for legal status, even if they qualified to do so through a relative or marriage, because they would be deported and denied entry for three years if they had been here without legal status for six months, and for ten years if they had been here without legal status for a year or more.

Defense of Marriage Act of 1996

In 1996, President Bill Clinton signed into law the **Defense of Marriage Act (DOMA)**, a bill introduced by Bob Barr (R-Ga). Section 3, which was eventually struck down, denied federal recognition of any marriage between same-sex couples, even if their marriage was deemed legal by their home state. Additionally, Section 2 of DOMA said that states do not have to acknowledge the marriages of same-sex couples who married in states where it was legal. This act made it impossible for same-sex couples to reap tax benefits that married couples enjoyed, and allowed states to refuse health insurance, adoption, and even death benefits to same-sex spouses.

> " As long as poverty, injustice and gross inequality persist in our world, none of us can truly rest. "
>
> **Nelson Mandela**
> South African anti-apartheid revolutionary

Personal Responsibility and Work Opportunity Reconciliation Act of 1996

Promising his detractors welfare reform, President Bill Clinton signed the **Personal Responsibility and Work Opportunity Reconciliation Act of 1996 (PRWORA)** which required welfare recipients to begin working after receiving assistance for two years. It also required that 25 percent of all families receiving assistance in each state be engaged in work activities. Furthermore, states were required to implement a child support enforcement program to crack down on non-paying parents.

The effects of this act were devastating, and due to the rising cost of childcare, many working families were thrust deeper into poverty. During this time, most welfare recipients were households headed by single mothers who now had to pay for childcare and transportation to work in order to fulfill the welfare requirements. They were forced to settle for jobs that barely paid enough to support their families. With wages of $6.00 to $8.00 an hour, their earnings were not enough to lift them out of poverty.

The *Terrorist Acts* of *2001* and the *Patriot Act*

On September 11, 2001, terrorists from Saudi Arabia associated with the Islamic extremist group al-Qaeda carried out a suicide attack against the United States. They hijacked four planes with the intention of using them as bombs. They flew two planes into the Twin Towers of the World Trade Center in New York City, and one plane into the Pentagon, just outside of Washington D.C. The fourth plane never reached its target, as its passengers fought back against the hijackers. The plane crashed in a field in Pennsylvania, killing all hijackers and all 45 passengers on board. One hundred and eighty-nine military personnel and civilians were killed at the Pentagon, including the passengers on the plane. In New York City, over 3,000 people died. Additionally, 343 firefighters and paramedics, 23 police officers, and 37 Port Authority police officers died while attempting to rescue people trapped in the buildings.

President George W. Bush vowed to make Osama bin Laden, who had orchestrated and financed the attacks, pay for these acts of terrorism. On October 7, 2001, Operation Enduring Freedom began, which in December 2001 successfully removed the Taliban from power in Afghanistan. However, the war continued, and forces moved into Pakistan.

Shortly after the 9/11 attacks, President George W. Bush signed the **Patriot Act of 2001**. While its stated intent was to catch terrorists, many believed that it criminalized everyday citizens. The act allows the FBI to obtain personal information on citizens without a warrant and does not require that information be destroyed, even upon proof of innocence. It also gives federal law enforcement agents the power to search a person's home with a warrant, without having to inform the owner until later. Additionally, the owner does not have to be present when the home is searched.

———— •◆• ————

The Rise of
Islamophobia
& the **2008** *Presidential Campaign*

Islamophobia is the unwarranted fear and hatred of those who practice the Islamic faith (Muslims). It is also a form of racism because, while there are many light-skinned Muslims, most are brown-skinned. While the anti-Muslim sentiment was not new, the 9/11 attacks were the beginning of widespread anti-Muslim sentiment in the United States. The media, as well as Christian fundamentalists, have played a part in perpetuating the idea that terrorism is synonymous with Islam.

In fact, while many White Americans can differentiate between extremist groups that claim to be Christian (such as the Ku Klux Klan) and peaceful followers of Christianity, they are unwilling to see the difference

" Is there something wrong with being a Muslim in this country? The answer is no. That's not America. **"**

Colin Powell
Retired 4-star General

between extremist groups that claim to be Islamic (such as al-Qaeda and Isis) and the millions of peaceful followers of Islam. The media bears some responsibility for supporting this narrative.

The true extent of this anti-Muslim sentiment and the reality of racism in America was reflected in the 2008 Presidential Campaign. At the time, Senator Barack Hussein Obama, a Black-identifying, biracial man from Illinois, was running against John McCain, a Senator and military hero from Arizona. Because Obama's middle name, Hussein, has Arabic origins and because his father was Kenyan, racist members of what became the Tea Party and the birther movement began to question the legitimacy of his American citizenship, something that would not have occurred had he been White-presenting. In fact, he was accused of being Muslim, as if practicing the Islamic faith automatically made him an enemy of the United States. Of those who demanded evidence of his citizenship, future President Donald Trump was one of the most vocal birthers.

This recession was the worst financial crisis since The Great Depression of 1929. In the early 2000s, the government, media, and financial advisors began to promote the "American Dream" of homeownership to the American people. Financial institutions, like Fannie Mae and Freddie Mac, started making government-backed mortgage loans to people who could not afford to pay them back. These mortgages were set up to be affordable options that allowed people with lower incomes to purchase homes without a down payment (a sum of cash that the buyer must pay at the time of purchase). For many potential homeowners of middle and lower incomes, the lack of a down payment can prevent them from being able to purchase a home. Not only were lenders offering mortgages without down payments, but they were also providing low-introductory interest rates (a fee based on the percentage of a loan). For the first eighteen months to two years, buyers would pay a minimal fee that would later increase.

Loan officers were receiving financial bonuses and incentives for making these deals, and they became very creative, by promising low interest rates on large sums of money. Many greedy loan officers convinced people to take out higher loans than they could afford based on the introductory interest rate. As lenders were closing these loans and investment firms were buying them, housing companies were building more houses than they could sell. That

caused a quick and drastic reduction in housing prices because the supply of homes became greater than the demand for them. As the introductory periods of these low-interest mortgages came to an end, many families found that they were unable to afford the new interest rates, which were often three to six times greater than their introductory rates. The interest increased their monthly mortgage payments and became a hardship. The solution for many was to try to refinance (borrow money against their homes) so that they would have money for living expenses. Rising interest rates and fees made this impossible, so many tried to sell their homes. At the same time, homeowners were defaulting on their loans at a much higher rate than the lending companies had expected. This increase in loan defaults caused some lenders, like Lehman Brothers, to go bankrupt and further increase interest rates.

Homeowners saw the value of their homes plummet. Selling would no longer cover the cost of their mortgage. When they were unable to sell and could no longer make their loan payments, the bank foreclosed (when a bank seizes ownership of property because its original owner has failed to make payments on the loan) on their homes. The influx of foreclosures caused an increase in homelessness and maxed out social service programs. Additionally, there were more homes available for purchase than there were buyers, which caused an economic crisis that companies responded to by laying off employees.

In response to the drastic economic decline, the U.S. Congress and President George W. Bush formulated and voted into action a financial bailout that gave $100 billion in taxpayer dollars to banks and mortgage lenders like Wells Fargo and Goldman Sachs. This allowed them to offset losses and remain in business. Many of the CEOs of these investment firms and banks used this money to pay out bonuses, even though they had, seemingly, robbed the American public. The recession lasted for two years, and the United States has not fully recovered. Across the board, families are poorer, job security is bleaker, and health care access is more difficult.

2.9 million properties went through foreclosure filings in 2010, or 2.23% of all housing units in the U.S.

Occupy [Wall Street] Protests

In September 2011, a group of protesters gathered in Zuccotti Park in New York City to address corporate greed, economic inequality, and corporate influence over the government and politicians. Inspired by similar protests that took place in Egypt and Tunisia, the movement was started and encouraged by a Canadian anti-consumerist magazine called *Adbusters*. With the goal of fighting back against the 1% (the population that holds most of the wealth in the United States), the initial **Occupy Wall Street (OWS)** protest sparked several similar movements across the United States and even internationally. Despite critics assuming that the participants in the OWS movement were young, unemployed college students, most were over 35 and employed. While the OWS movement splintered into subgroups, it did serve to mobilize many who wanted to affect change but felt helpless. It also helped to encourage the creation of other movements such as the Fight for $15, which works to increase the minimum wage to a living wage of $15 per hour.

Violence Against & Murder of Black Americans

with Impunity

Since 1980, the killing of unarmed Black women, men, and children has become more public in large part due to the advancements in technology. We are now able to record incidents or go live to reach a broader audience. These advancements have not made it easier to find justice when police kill Black people.

Murder with impunity - or without legal repercussion - is an essential cause of movements such as **Black Lives Matter**. Seeing images of murdered Black bodies plastered on the news and social media sites makes it hard for many Black people to feel safe. Moreover, the conversations that Black parents must have with their children to keep them safe are heartbreaking. However, it is the reality for far too many.

What many of these cases have in common is that police officers are acting out of fear and are choosing to unleash uncontrolled violence rather than attempting to de-escalate the situation. Their victims, in most cases, have been unarmed and have not committed crimes.

A note from the author: *I have included a few cases where Black people were murdered or beaten by police and/or vigilantes, knowing two things to be true:*

(1) there are far too many cases for me to include them all.
(2) While not all police officers are racist and violent, racism and fear of Black and Brown people is ingrained in the culture of the police force. We need to address it.

This section is a difficult one to read and a tough one to discuss. As you read through this section, don't hesitate to take a break or to do some research.

Rodney King & the Los Angeles Riots of 1992

On March 3, 1991, Rodney King was violently beaten by Laurence Powell, Timothy Wind, and Theodore Briseno, three White Los Angeles police officers, while their supervisor, Stacey Koon, watched. The beating was videotaped by a witness, George Holiday, and showed the officers surrounding and striking King repeatedly. King was unarmed. The officers stomped, kicked, and beat him with batons. None of the other officers did anything to stop the beating. While this was not the first incident of police brutality within the Black community, it was the first time there was video footage offering proof of the racist, inhuman treatment committed by police that the Black community had been reporting for more than two decades. This was before smartphones, YouTube, or Facebook Live, so recording this incident was an improbable feat.

Because of the footage, the three police officers were charged with assault with a deadly weapon and excessive use of force, and their supervisor was charged with aiding and abetting. Additionally, Powell and Koon were charged with filing a false police report. For many, the case seemed to be open and shut. Yet, despite the glaring example of out-of-control behavior, the officers were acquitted of all charges by a predominately White jury. Still, an independent commission found that the Los Angeles Police Department engaged in a culture of violence, racism, and corruption.

Rodney King was awarded $3.8 million in a separate lawsuit against the city of Los Angeles, and went on to become engaged to Cynthia Kelley, one of the female jurors of that trial.

Feeling hopeless and angry, members of marginalized communities of Los Angeles took to the streets in protest, which quickly escalated to riots that lasted three days. Police officers took their time responding to the violence, and when they did, they focused only on patrolling the borders of the more affluent neighborhoods rather than on trying to stop the riots where they were happening. On May 1, 1992, President George H.W. Bush dispatched military troops and federal officers to Los Angeles to help bring the city under control. In that time, there were more than 60 deaths and over one billion dollars in damages. For many Black Americans and other people of color in the United States, the acquittal of the police officers was further evidence that racism was alive and actively working against them. It was also proof that the legal system would not hold accountable those responsible for the inhumane treatment of Black people.

The Murder of Amadou Diallo

◆

On February 4, 1999, Amadou Diallo, an immigrant from the country of Guinea, in Africa, was shot and killed by four police officers in the Bronx, NY. The four police officers were members of the New York Street Crimes unit - a group tasked with finding illegal guns and arresting those responsible for selling and distributing them.

The officers stopped Diallo because he matched the description of a serial rapist who was previously active in the area. They asked him to show them his hands, and he either ran or walked away. He reached into his pocket, and one police officer thought he had a gun. The cops fired forty-nine bullets and hit Diallo nineteen times.

A grand jury indicted the officers, and this case became a glaring example of the horrors of Mayor Giuliani's "Stop and Frisk" program, in which officers detain citizens they believe are guilty of a crime even when there is no reasonable suspicion. Activist Rev. Al Sharpton, former Mayor David Dinkins, and Democratic supporters marched, rallied, and advocated for reform. However, the police officers were not convicted.

◆

" I was stunned by the verdict. It shows that racial profiling seeps so deeply in our society that a wallet in the hand of a white man looks like a wallet and the wallet in the hand of a black man looks like a gun. **"**

Bill Bradley

2000 Democratic presidential candidate

The Murder of Rekia Boyd

On March 21, 2012, Rekia Boyd and a group of friends gathered at an intersection in Chicago after leaving a party. Dante Servin, an off-duty police officer who had just called in a noise complaint about the party, approached the group and told them to keep it down. Some harsh words were exchanged and Servin fired an unregistered weapon into the group from his car. A bullet hit Rekia Boyd in the head, and she died a few days later. Servin claimed that one of the other group members approached his car and had a gun but police did not recover a weapon. Rekia Boyd was twenty-two.

A grand jury indicted Servin on charges of involuntary manslaughter, but he was cleared of all charges when the judge ruled that he could not be charged with recklessness (required for involuntary manslaughter). Because the shooting was intentional, the charge should have been first-degree murder.

The Murder of
Trayvon Martin
February, 2012

Trayvon Martin was a 17-year-old Black American high school student who was fatally shot by George Zimmerman, a 28-year-old White-identifying Hispanic man who served as the neighborhood watch coordinator. Zimmerman had a history of making numerous complaints to the police about people in the neighborhood, focusing mainly on the race of the assumed perpetrator.

Martin was staying at the home of his father's fiancé at The Retreat, a community in Twin Lakes, Florida. As Martin was returning home after purchasing items at a

local convenience store, Zimmerman called the police to report a suspicious, unknown male walking around the neighborhood. While on the phone with the dispatcher, Zimmerman began to chase Trayvon Martin, despite the dispatcher's insistence that he not do that. After hanging up, Zimmerman had what he called a violent encounter with Trayvon Martin, whom he fatally shot. Martin was about 70 yards from his back door. Zimmerman, who had a bloody nose and cuts on the back of his head, claimed that he shot Martin in self-defense under Florida's **Stand Your Ground** statute. Under the law, those who claim self-defense cannot be arrested unless there is evidence to contradict that claim. George Zimmerman did stand trial for second-degree murder but was acquitted of the charges, as there was no evidence to dispute his account of the events that led to Martin's death.

Media coverage surrounding this incident was not kind to Trayvon Martin. Fox host Geraldo Rivera accused Martin, who had been wearing a hoodie, of dressing like a gangster. Rivera accused Martin of being just as responsible as Zimmerman for his own death. He even asked parents of color to keep their children from wearing hoodies to prevent their deaths. Respectability politics came into focus as the media and conservatives called for marginalized groups to behave, do what they were told, and to stay within mainstream values in order to avoid death. Humanity would only be granted to those who dressed, spoke, and behaved in ways that were not overtly ethnic or fringe.

Many Americans were outraged. Martin's mother created a petition on Change.org calling for Zimmerman's arrest. The petition collected 2.2 million signatures. Protests broke out across the country in response to the shooting. The entire Miami Heat NBA team wore hoodies in support and remembrance of Trayvon Martin. Many Florida high school students staged walkouts. The Occupy Wall Street movement marched in support and in memory of Martin during the Million Hoodie March in New York City. Additionally, President Barack Obama and civil right leaders Reverend Jesse Jackson and Reverend Al Sharpton called for a thorough investigation into the shooting. Trayvon Martin's death conjured up images of the death of Emmett Till, a 14-year-old Black boy from Chicago, who was murdered in 1955 after a White woman lied and said that he had inappropriately spoken to her. Till was hunted down, kidnapped, and brutally murdered by the woman's husband and his half-brother. Like Zimmerman, Till's killers were acquitted of his murder.

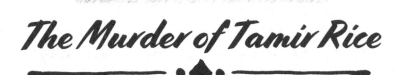

The Murder of Tamir Rice

Tamir Rice, a twelve-year-old Black boy, was playing with a toy gun in a Cleveland, Ohio park in November 2012. Someone called 911 and reported that there was a Black male pointing a gun at people, but said that the gun was probably fake and that the Black male was probably a young person. The dispatcher asked twice if the person was Black or White. Moreover, when she put the call out to on-duty officers, she left out that the gun was probably fake and that the male was probably a juvenile.

When officers Timothy Loehmann and Frank Garmback arrived on the scene, they asked Tamir to "show them" his hands, but when Loehmann believed Tamir was pulling a gun out of his waistband, he shot him twice. Neither officer administered first aid to Tamir, who had taken two bullets. It was four minutes before another officer and an FBI agent arrived on the scene and began treating the boy.

A Grand Jury failed to indict either officer, as Tamir Rice had what looked like a real gun.

Experts discovered that the gun was missing the orange marking that should identify it as a toy. It was discovered that Loehmann had two years earlier resigned from the Independence, Ohio Police Department rather than be fired. Independence Deputy Police Chief, Jim Polak, said that Loehmann had been unable to follow basic instructions and cited a "dangerous loss of composure" in a weapons training class. On his application for the Cleveland Police Department, Loehmann claimed that he had left Independence for "personal reasons" and Cleveland police never reviewed his personnel file from Independence before hiring him.

In the aftermath of the shooting, the media blamed Tamir Rice's mother for giving her son the toy gun, although it had actually been given to him by a friend minutes before the shooting. The media called Tamir "scary" and a police chief in Miami called him a "thug."

But Tamir Rice was twelve years old.

On August 9, 2014, 18-year-old Michael Brown Jr. was shot by Darren Wilson, a White police officer in Ferguson, Missouri, after Brown allegedly stole some items from a local convenience store. Brown was unarmed and was reportedly holding his hands up when he was shot. A high school graduate, Brown was about to begin a heating and air conditioning repair training program at Vatterott College.

After his murder, Michael Brown, who had been shot twice in the head and at least six more times elsewhere, was left uncovered for hours. The dehumanization of yet another Black person was on full display. The Department of Justice cleared Wilson of any wrongdoing because he stated that he shot Brown in self-defense, but Brown's friend, Dorian Johnson, who was with him that night, has maintained that his friend's hands were up in surrender when Wilson shot him.

Protests formed as the citizens of Ferguson brought attention to the years of racial bias by police officers. The number one criticism was that Brown was considered a threat and that deadly force was used immediately. There was no attempt to subdue him or to de-escalate the situation. Instead, Wilson chose to murder a suspect who "matched the description" - a reason that has been used countless times to kill Black people. Additionally, the stark contrast in the treatment of Black vs. White suspects is further proof that continued systemic racism threatens the lives of all Black people. Just months after Michael Brown Jr.'s murder, the Department of Justice reported that for years the police department of Ferguson, Missouri, had engaged in unchecked racial bias.

The Murder of
Michael Brown Jr.
Ferguson, Missouri
2014

The Death of Sandra Bland

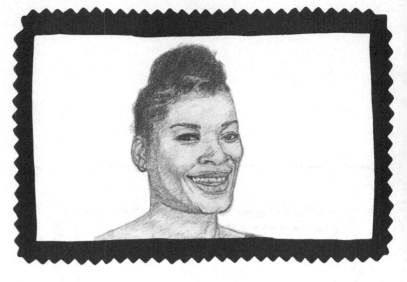

In July 2015, three days after being arrested in Texas by Brian Encinia, Sandra Bland was found dead in her jail cell, a victim of alleged suicide. A bystander recorded her arrest, and some of it was captured on the officer's dashcam. Encinia stopped Bland for failing to signal when changing lanes, but the arrest became confrontational when the officer demanded that Bland extinguish the cigarette she was smoking in her car, despite not being under arrest. She was forcibly removed from her vehicle, slammed to the ground and feared that her arm had been broken. What led to her death was a combination of neglect on behalf of the Texas Department of Public Safety and the trauma of being a Black woman in the United States.

In the four years since Sandra Bland had graduated from college, she struggled to find work, which resulted in an inability to pay for basic needs. She faced numerous fines stemming from traffic violations and possession of marijuana. She relied on a family friend for support and had been self-medicating with marijuana and alcohol, as she could not afford healthcare to treat her depression or epilepsy. Bland also suffered an ectopic pregnancy and the death of a maternal figure, both within three days of each other. She had also become increasingly saddened by the repeated traumas that she and other Black people had endured at the hands of police.

After her arrest, Bland disclosed to officers that she was depressed and feeling suicidal. Instead of receiving the care that she needed, they placed her alone in a cell. Unable to make contact with her family members or raise the $550 bond that she needed to be released, Sandra pleaded with police officers to allow her to make free calls to family, but they denied her requests and told her to use the pay phone that charged those called $14.99. Her family was struggling financially, and Bland did not want to burden them further. She died alone and afraid.

Sandra Bland's death raised awareness of not only the problems with the criminal justice system and the lack of adherence to regulations put in place to ensure that those arrested are kept safe, but it also shed light on the trauma of being Black in America. From seeing numerous police officers go unpunished after killing Black suspects, to the strong Black woman stereotype that depicts Black women as super-human and able to endure pain and suffering without emotional strain, Black people are suffering from Post-Traumatic Stress Disorder and depression at alarming rates.

The Death of
Kalief Browder

Sixteen-year-old Kalief Browder was accused of stealing a backpack when a man called police about the theft and then identified Browder and his friend. The victim's story changed many times - he initially claimed that Browder and his friend robbed him earlier that day but later said it had been a week earlier. Browder insisted on his innocence but remained in custody on Rikers Island for three years, awaiting a trial that never took place. He spent two years in solitary confinement and during his three years of incarceration on the island, he endured numerous beatings by both guards and inmates.

Browder tried to commit suicide numerous times while incarcerated and continued to do so once released in 2013. Not only did he suffer physically, but mentally as well. He became paranoid and restless, suffered panic attacks, and struggled to complete classes at Bronx Community College where he was enrolled. While the publicity surrounding his case got the attention of several celebrities and politicians, it did little to ease his suffering. In 2015, Browder died by suicide.

The Kalief Browder case brought to light the horrible conditions of not only Rikers Island but American prisons overall. In interviews, Kalief spoke about having to wash his clothes by hand, being starved and denied medical care, and receiving numerous beatings by guards and gang members. His case also provided insight into the inefficient court system. Simple cases like Browder's take too long to close and what often results is a miscarriage of justice and the denial of a speedy trial - a right guaranteed by the United States Constitution.

The Murder of Philando Castile

In July 2016, Philando Castile, a thirty-two-year-old man who was loved by parents and teachers alike at the elementary school where he worked as a supervisor in the cafeteria, was shot and killed by Jeronimo Yanez, a police officer working with the Minnesota Police Department. Philando, his girlfriend, Diamond Reynolds, and her four-year-old daughter were stopped for a traffic violation. Upon being asked for his license and registration, Castile informed the officer that he had a licensed gun and reached for his documents as instructed. Yanez shot him seven times despite there being a child in the car. He claimed that Castile was reaching for the firearm, but the gun was still in Castile's pocket when he was placed in the ambulance. Philando Castile died twenty minutes after being shot.

Reynolds filmed the event as it occurred and posted the video on Facebook Live. Viewers could see Castile slumped over in the driver's seat. Reynolds was told to get on her knees and was handcuffed. She and her daughter were placed in a squad car, and on the dashcam we hear the four-year-old girl telling her mom "Mom, please stop cussing and screaming 'cause I don't want you to get shooted."

Yanez 's reasons for the initial stop have been inconsistent. At first, he said that he pulled Castile over because he and Reynolds matched the description of two suspects in an armed robbery. Those suspects were said to be Black men with shoulder-length dreadlocks. He later said that he stopped them for a broken tail-light. Yanez also claimed to see the gun in Philando Castile's hand.

Public outcry over the events spread quickly, in large part due to the Facebook Live video. Governor Mark Dayton spoke to the residents of Minnesota and called the murder unacceptable, promising justice. But justice was not served. Yanez was found not guilty of manslaughter and reckless discharge of a firearm, despite the inconsistencies in his testimony. He was removed from the police force but received a monetary payout that would allow for him to transition into a new career.

Diamond Reynolds received an $800,000 settlement for the emotional distress and false arrest that occurred the night Castile was murdered. Philando Castile's family also received a settlement of $3 million.

" This is not just a black issue. It's not just a Hispanic issue. This is an American issue. "

Barack Obama
44th U.S. President

The Murder of Korryn Gaines

On August 1, 2016, Baltimore police officers arrived at Korryn Gaines' apartment to serve her with a misdemeanor bench warrant for failure to appear in court and also to serve her boyfriend with a warrant for a domestic violence charge that Gaines had brought against him. When she refused to open the door, police stormed in. Her boyfriend surrendered with his one-year-old child, but his other son ran back to his mother, Gaines, and refused to leave.

When officers entered the apartment, they found Korryn seated on the floor and pointing a gun at them. Her five-year-old son was also in the apartment. During a six-hour standoff, Gaines used Facebook Live to report on what was happening in her apartment, until Facebook deactivated her account at the police department's request. Gaines was traumatized by the news coverage of repeated murders and killings of Black people by police and feared for her life when coming into contact with them. She reacted the way she did out of fear for her safety and the safety of her child.

Gaines' mother arrived at the scene. Police then used her cell phone to call Gaines but did not allow her mother to intervene or talk to Korryn. Additionally, Baltimore's Mobile Crisis Team was not dispatched, and there was no mental health clinician on the scene to help de-escalate the situation. Instead, police used aggressive force to enter the apartment and ultimately killed Gaines and injured her son.

While the police deemed the shooting justifiable, Korryn Gaines' family was awarded $37 million in damages when a jury agreed that Corporal Royce Ruby, the officer who fired the shot that killed Gaines, violated Korryn's and her son's civil rights.

The Massacre at Emanuel

African American
Methodist Episcopal Church

Names of the Deceased

The Rev. Daniel Simmons

Age 72. Retired pastor and teacher.

Cynthia Graham Hurd

Age 54. Manager of the St. Andrews Regional Library.

Ethel Lance

Age 70. Retired housekeeper at Gaillard Auditorium.

The Rev. Depayne Middleton-Doctor

Age 49. Admissions Coordinator at Southern Wesleyan.

Tywanza Sanders

Age 26. Poet, artist, and barber planning to attend graduate school.

Myra Thompson

Age 59. Retired school teacher and member of Delta Sigma Theta Sorority.

The Rev. Sharonda Singleton

Age 45. Speech-Language Pathologist and head coach of the girl's track team. Mother of three.

Susie Jackson

Age 87. Choir member and grandmother.

The Rev. Clementa Pinckney

Age 41. Pastor, State Senator.

The Emanuel African Methodist Episcopal Church in Charleston, South Carolina was founded in part by Denmark Vessey, a freedman who was accused of and executed for planning a slave revolt in 1822. The church has had a long history of hosting Black civil rights' leaders, from Booker T. Washington to Reverend Dr. Martin Luther King, Jr.

On June 17, 2015, a twenty-one-year-old White man opened fire on a group of Black people attending Bible study at the church. This act of domestic terrorism took place in Charleston, South Carolina, and was carried out by White supremacist, Dylann Roof, because he wanted to start a race war. Unfortunately, it was not the first time that White supremacists and hate groups targeted a Black church.

The loss of life was horrific. However, the way that the police and the media handled Roof in the aftermath of the shooting stands in stark contrast to what happens when suspects are Black. Not only was he provided a bullet-proof vest before being walked outside to the police cars, he was also given a hamburger once in custody. While this is not exactly five-star treatment, because he was detained peacefully after being suspected of multiple homicides, it called attention to the disparity in the actions of police when suspects are not White.

For example, in 2016, Korryn Gaines (*page 48*) was shot and killed when police stormed her home because she would not answer when they came to serve a warrant. The same year, Philando Castile (*page 47*) was shot during what was supposed to be a routine traffic stop. In 1991, Rodney King (*page 38*), who was also unarmed, was beaten during an arrest and in 1999, Amadou Diallo (*page 39*) was shot and killed by police when they mistook him for a rape suspect.

The media was also kinder to Roof, an alleged murderer, than they were to Trayvon Martin, who was a victim. Martin was called a thug for wearing a hoodie, a term that does not invoke sympathy. Roof, on the other hand, was painted as a troubled young man whose life was made difficult by his parents' divorce and his mother's financial instability.

Right: the Emmanuel African American Methodist Episcopal Church.

Modern Era
Movements & Leaders

Civil Rights Then and Now

Black Lives Matter

In response to the acquittal of George Zimmerman for the murder of Trayvon Martin and the dehumanization of Martin by the media, Alicia Garza, Patrisse Cullors, and Opal Tometi created the hashtag and call-to-action **#BlackLivesMatter**. The focus of the movement is to affirm the vibrant contributions of Black people to American culture, to reaffirm the humanity of Black Americans, and to organize to affect change by revitalizing the Black Liberation Movement and fight against the systemic oppression, racism, and murder of Black people in the United States. It is important to note that while the original movement began online, Black Lives Matter, as an official organization and team lead by Alicia, Patrisse, and Opal, has become a physical movement that organizes events and actions.

"Right now, when we're hearing so much disturbing and hateful rhetoric, it is so important to remember that our diversity has been - and will always be - our greatest source of strength and pride here in the United States."

Michelle Obama
Former First Lady

Bree Newsome, Activist

A few weeks after the tragic murders of nine people at Emanuel African Methodist Episcopal church, Bree Newsome, a thirty-year-old activist, filmmaker, and artist, scaled the thirty-foot flagpole outside the South Carolina statehouse and removed a symbol of racism, hate, and oppression: the Confederate flag.

While the police arrested Newsome, her actions helped spark a conversation about systemic racism and the removal of all symbols that honor the Confederacy. Many White people in the South believe that the flag is representative of American history, but for Black people, the flag symbolizes a South so invested in the system of slavery that they would rather secede from the Union than dismantle the institution. With the flag and monuments honoring Confederate soldiers decorating public spaces and in government buildings, Black people are reminded that this country is not a safe space for those with brown skin.

" The Lord is my light and my salvation, whom shall I fear? "
Quote from the Bible
Spoken by Bree Newsome regarding her act

Tarana Burke

In 2006, Tarana Burke, an American Civil Rights activist, began using the phrase "**Me Too**" on Twitter to raise awareness about sexual assault and sexual abuse. The phrase was something that she wished she had said to other survivors of sexual assault so that they knew that they were not alone. She created Just Be, Inc. to help promote mental and physical wellness amongst marginalized women and young girls.

The goal of "Me Too" is to help young women of color from low-wealth communities heal from sexual assault through empathy and by providing resources to help facilitate their healing. While the "me too" movement gained popularity when actresses began coming forward with their experiences in Hollywood, the focus of the movement has and continues to be on Black, Indigenous, and People of Color (BIPOC) who are often more likely to endure sexual assault.

Along with others, Tarana Burke was named "Person of the Year" in 2017 by Time Magazine. As the Senior Director of the non-profit **Girls for Gender Equality (GGE)** in Brooklyn, New York, she continues to help create opportunities for young BIPOC to overcome the many hurdles that they face. Through GGE, Ms. Burke tackles issues of sexism, poverty, racial injustices, transphobia, homophobia, and harassment.

Landmark
Cases & Amendments
from the 1980s to 2015

In 1975, Texas reworked their education laws to deny local school districts funding for providing education to children of undocumented immigrants. The U.S. Supreme Court ruled that this new law violated the 14th Amendment's Equal Protection Clause because, despite their immigrant status, they were entitled to protection under the 14th Amendment, and Texas could not deny their right to education. The Court stated that Texas was unable to prove that the revision was needed. They struck down the law.

Wygant v. Jackson Board of Education
1986

Plyler v. Doe
1982

The Court ruled that affirmative action provisions should address the problems caused by prior discriminatory hiring practices. In this case, an agreement between the Board of Education and the teachers' union that required a percentage of minority teachers be exempt from layoff to provide role models for the minority students, did not address previous practices. Instead, it created a situation of "separate but equal," which was previously deemed unlawful in **Brown v. Board of Education**.

The Court ruled that The Alabama Department of Public Safety action plan to reserve half of the department's promotions for qualified Black officers did not violate the 14th Amendment's Equal Protection Clause because it did not prevent White officers from advancing. In fact, the plan only covered specific roles in the department. The Court ruled that the 14th Amendment's protection did not cover the promotion plan, and that in light of the Department's past racist practices, the plan was necessary.

The Court ruled that the Constitution does not protect the rights of LGBTQ individuals to engage in acts of intimacy (termed sodomy), thus validating state laws outlawing this conduct.

United States v. Paradise
1987

Bowers v. Hardwick
1987

Meritor Savings Bank v. Vinson
1986

The Court unanimously ruled that the **Civil Rights Act** not only protected men and women from economic and tangible discrimination but that it also covered the entire spectrum of ill-treatment in the workplace. They determined that Title VII does apply to sexual harassment, as it is a form of sex discrimination, which causes an abusive or hostile work environment, but they declined to rule on the degree that a company is liable for the actions of its employees.

Landmark Cases & Amendments

The Court ruled the Santa Ana Transportation Agency's promotion process did not violate Title VII, as considering the sex of an applicant is one of many factors in the decision process and does not bar men from being promoted.

A group of White unskilled employees filed a suit against The Wards Cove Packing Company, which employed mostly non-white unskilled workers in their seasonal canning positions. The Supreme Court ruled that a disparity alone did not constitute discrimination and that evidence would need to be presented that demonstrates how hiring practices violate Title VII.

Johnson v. Transportation Agency
1987

Lyng v. Northwest Indian Cemetery Protection
1989

Wards Cove Packing Co. Inc. v. Antonio
1989

The Northwest Indian Cemetery Protective Association challenged the harvesting of trees to build a road that would cut through grounds held sacred by many Native American communities. The Supreme Court deemed that government could not operate if they had to appeal to every citizen's religious needs and that the 1st Amendment did not provide protection from government programs that were not prohibiting religious practices. In this case, though the harvesting would destroy the area where religious activities occurred, it did not stop anyone from practicing their religion.

Civil Rights Then and Now

When Colorado passed Amendment 2 of the Colorado State Constitution, which removed protections designed to protect the rights and practices of the Lesbian, Gay, and Bisexual community in all judicial, legislative, or executive actions, an appeal was filed in the U.S. Supreme Court. The Court ruled that Amendment 2 did violate the 14th Amendment's Equal Protection Clause by targeting a segment of the community to deny their rights and remove their ability to take action in the courts.

When Dr. Bragdon refused to treat Sidney Abbott at his office, offering to treat her at a hospital for no extra cost because she was HIV positive, Abbott sued, claiming that the dentist had discriminated against her based on her health status. Both a federal and appellate court sided with Sidney Abbott, but Dr. Bragdon appealed to the U.S. Supreme Court. The Court heard his case and concluded that because Abbott was not posing a direct health threat, Dr. Bragdon was, in fact, discriminating against her, and was in violation of the **Americans With Disabilities Act (ADA)**.

Bragdon v. Abbott
1997

Romer v. Evans
1996

Olmstead v. L.C.
1999

The Atlanta Legal Aid Society, acting on behalf of two female mental patients, sued Tommy Olmstead, the Commissioner of the Georgia Department of Human Resources, for the Georgia Regional Hospital's decision to keep the women in isolation, despite having been cleared to receive integrated treatment and be moved to a more communal setting. Olmstead argued that the decision was based on a lack of financial resources. The Supreme Court, however, ruled that a lack of funds should not determine whether states comply with Title II of the 1990 **Americans With Disabilities Act**, unless the state can show that allocation of resources to one patient will cause harm to others.

The Court ruled that there was no justification for Texas to intrude into the personal and intimate lives of consenting adults, even if they are same-sex couples. To that end, arresting adults for engaging in consensual, intimate acts was a violation of liberty under the Due Process Clause.

17-year-old Christopher Simmons was sentenced to death after being convicted of murder. The Supreme Court, however, ruled, that the execution of minors (those younger than twenty-one) is cruel and unusual punishment and is prohibited by the 8th Amendment of the U.S. Constitution.

Lawrence v. Texas
2003

Roper v. Simmons
2005

Arizona v. Inter Tribal Council of Arizona
2013

The Court ruled that Proposition 200, passed on November 2, 2004, in Arizona, which required voters to provide proof of citizenship when registering to vote and when voting, violated the **National Voter Registration Act of 1993 (NVRA)**.

The Green family are the owners and operators of Hobby Lobby Stores, Inc., a national arts and crafts supply chain. They argued that requiring employers to provide contraception and preventative care under the **Patient Protection and Affordable Care Act (ACA)** violated their rights under the Free Exercise Clause of the 1st Amendment and the **Religious Freedom Restoration Act of 1993 (RFRA)**. Because the family chooses to run their business based on their interpretation of the Bible, they believed that employment-based group health care plans that provide birth control were anti-Christian. The Supreme Court ruled that the Religious Freedom Restoration Act of 1993 granted closely-held for-profit corporations the right to decide against paying for services to which they held religious objections. However, the Court also ruled that this decision only applied to the contraceptive regulations of the ACA, and nothing else.

" This decision affirms what millions of Americans already believe in their hearts: when all Americans are treated as equal we are all more free. "

Barack Obama
44th US President

Obergefell v Hodges
2015

Burwell v. Hobby Lobby Stores, Inc.
2014

When several groups of same-sex couples from Tennessee, Michigan, Ohio, and Kentucky challenged the state's laws that didn't recognize their marriages from states where it was legal, the Court ruled that marriage is one of the fundamental liberties guaranteed by the 14th Amendment, which applies to same-sex couples in the same way that it does to opposite-sex couples. The Court also stated that the exclusion of same-sex couples from the right to marry violated the Due Process Clause of the 14th Amendment and while the 1st Amendment allows religious institutions to adhere to their principles, it does not grant states the right to deny same-sex couples the right to marry in the same legal way as opposite-sex couples.

In Summary
of Civil Rights Then & Now

Whew! That was a lot of information, and we've left out so much. The struggle for civil liberties is an ongoing process and one that has been met with frustration from those who are either unwilling, or too ill-informed, to see how systemic discrimination continues to diminish the greatness of the United States. The truth is that while it seems like there has been a lot of progress since the earliest incarnations of the Civil Rights Movement, the continued murder of Black women, men, and children, the continued bashing of the those who do not fit the mainstream definition of what is acceptable, and a government that seems to listen more to money than to its people, has caused a regression of many of our accomplishments. Between biased, misleading, and often untrue news, politicians who seek to divide and promote hate, and the decline in a well-rounded educational system, it has become harder to unify people under a common goal.

...
So, what now?

How do we continue to fight to ensure that no one is suffering under a system of oppression?

There are no easy answers. What is evident is that we all must fight. Complacency and neutrality are no longer options. Injustices must be met with anger from Black and White people alike. Furthermore, in a system that favors Whiteness, heterosexuality, and maleness, those who must carry the weight of dismantling the system will be those who most benefit from it. We must remember that none of us can be free if that freedom comes from the oppression of others. Get involved! Learn to put kindness and empathy first. When possible, stand up for those who are being oppressed. Don't be silent!

It's a start.

Questions
for Comprehension

Multiple Choice

1. The purpose of the bailout that gave $100 billion in taxpayer dollars to banks and lenders was to:

    A. Give bonuses to lenders and CEOs.
    B. Allow them to stay in business so that they did not have to lay off employees.
    C. Provide extra money for borrowers so that they could take time to pay back their mortgages.
    D. Keep the crisis quiet so no one knew how bad it really was.

2. Zimmerman justified the killing of Trayvon Martin under what Florida law?

    A. Jim Crow
    B. Citizen's Arrest
    C. Stand Your Ground
    D. Any Means Necessary

3. Barack Hussein Obama is NOT (circle all that apply)

    A. An observer of Islam
    B. The first Black-Identifying President of the United States
    C. An American citizen
    D. A terrorist

4. Kalief Browder was imprisoned for three years because:

    A. He was found guilty of a crime
    B. He pleaded guilty to a crime and was sentenced
    C. He was denied the right to a speedy trial
    D. He was a threat to the public

True or False

5. _____ The Civil Liberties Act of 1998 apologized to Black People for over three-hundred years of slavery and racism.

6. _____ HIV is the result of drug use and sexuality.

7. _____ The modern Civil Rights Movement utilizes social media as well as community organizing.

8. _____ Undocumented child-immigrants are allowed to receive an education in public schools.

Fill in the Blanks

9. The Supreme Court ruled in _____ that sentencing a minor to death is cruel and unusual punishment.

10. The terrorist attacks of September 11, 2001 were orchestrated by religious _____ who are not representative of most who practice Islam.

11. Sandra Bland's death may have been the result of _____, which can be due to the trauma of repeated exposure to racism, discrimination, and systemic oppression that causes financial strain.

12. The "Me Too" movement was created by _____ as a way to raise awareness about sexual assault and sexual abuse.

Short Answer Questions

13. Why did it become more difficult to fight against racism and discrimination in the decades following the Civil Rights Movement of the 1960s?

14. What is a major difference between the Civil Rights Movement of 1960s and the Modern Civil Rights Movement?

15. What effects did the War on Drugs have on marginalized communities?

16. Why was the outcome of the trials of the officers accused of beating Rodney King a blow to Black communities?

17. What were some of the common experiences of those living with HIV and/or AIDS?

18. In what ways did the Supreme Court cases about civil rights violations become more difficult?

19. How did police treatment of domestic terrorist, Dylann Roof, represent the disparity between the way Black and White suspects are treated by police?

20. Social media continues to play a large role in community organizing. What are some ways that people have used it as a tool?

Answers found on Page 70

Overall Discussion & Essay Questions

Overall Essay Questions

1. Based on what you have read, create a Venn Diagram comparing and contrasting the issues of importance igniting the Civil Rights Movement of the 1960s and those of the present-day movement.

2. It has been said that we currently live in a "post-racial society," or a society that no longer prioritizes race when judging both individuals and groups of people. Do you agree? Why or why not?

3. Most civil rights activities during the 1960s were in-person events. Methods included protesting, boycotting, sit-ins, and local organizing. Much has changed in modern day society. Compare and contrast one 1960s initiative mentioned in Part 1 to a more recent one mentioned in Part 2. Discuss the catalyst for the initiatives and how marginalized communities organized, protested, and changed things for the better.

4. Have you noticed examples of discrimination in your everyday life? What are some ways that you can prevent these things from happening?

5. What are the similarities between the murders of Trayvon Martin and Emmett Till?

6. How are the advances made by Black Americans in the areas of civil rights beneficial for other marginalized groups of people?

7. In your own words, define the purpose of the following:
   - The Movement for Black Lives
   - The Black Panther Movement
   - Occupy Wall Street
   - Montgomery Bus Boycott

8. If you could talk to President Trump about the state of race relations in this country, what would you say?

9. How important is it for the United States to be open to immigrants? In what ways is immigration beneficial?

10. Religious freedom means the right to practice your religion (or not, if you don't want to). In what ways does Islamophobia deny religious freedom?

11. How did the Clinton administration contribute to the rise in prison population?

12. In what ways can you change yourself to ensure that you are more inclusive and open to the differences of others?

Activities

13. What does diversity mean to you? Create a poster of what a diverse world would look like.

14. Are you confused about any topic covered in this book? Talk about them with your parent or teacher (or child or students) and research them further.

15. How many works of fiction have you read by non-White and non-Christian authors? Challenge yourself to read at least ten (10) new books. You can start with our Recommended Reading list.

Glossary

Abolish (v)
to end or do away with

Abolitionist (n)
a person who advocated the end of slavery and the freeing of all slaves

Acquired Immune Deficiency Syndrome (AIDS) (n)
a serious disease of the human immune system caused by the HIV infection

Affirmative Action (n)
a policy of promoting opportunities for members of groups that have previously experienced discrimination

Amendment (n)
a change or addition to a document

Bias (n)
inclination or prejudice for or against one person or group, especially in a way considered to be unfair

Biracial (adj.)
having parents who are of two races

Chattel (n)
personal property

Civil Rights (n)
rights to full legal, social, and economic equality

Complacency (n)
the act of enjoying quiet pleasure while ignoring or being unaware of danger; satisfaction of existing in current situation

Desegregation (n)
the elimination of laws that allowed for segregation

Emancipation Proclamation (n)
An executive order issued by Abraham Lincoln on January 1, 1863, which freed slaves in the 13 slave states still involved in the rebellion against the Union (the Civil War). It also allowed freed slaves to join the Union Army and be paid for their service. While it freed slaves, the Emancipation Proclamation did not make slavery illegal.

Equal Protection Clause
part of the 14th Amendment that prevents states from denying any man equal protection of its laws

Equality (n)
uniform and balanced treatment

Extremist (n)
someone who believes in fanatical religious or political views

Freedman (n)
an emancipated slave

Fundamentalist (adj.)

advocating for the strict, literal interpretation of a religious doctrine

Homelessness (n)

the state of not having a home or a permanent place of residence

Human Immunodeficiency Virus (HIV) (n)

a group of viruses that infect and destroy helper T-cells, causing a significant reduction in their numbers; the virus that can lead to AIDS, HIV is transmitted through the exchange of bodily fluids

Inalienable Rights (n)

rights that are granted by nature or God and that cannot be taken away

Inequality (n)

lack of consistency in treatment, opportunity, or representation between different groups or individuals

Inflation (n)

a continual increase in the price of goods and services

Infringe (v)

to violate or break the terms of an agreement

Jim Crow (n)

a practice or policy of segregating or discriminating against Black people, as in public places, public vehicles, or employment

Ku Klux Klan (n)

a terrorist organization that advocates for, and participates in, extremist activities centered around hatred towards anyone who is not White and Christian

Legal (adj)

made right by law

LGBTQ (acronym)

Lesbian, Gay, Bisexual, Transgender, and Queer (or Questioning)

Living Wage (n)

an earned wage that is high enough for a worker to maintain a standard of living in which a family's basic needs can be met

Mainstream America (adj)

ordinary American people who are not ethnically or culturally marginalized (White, heterosexual, abled, wealthy, skinny, etc.)

Marginalize (v)

to put in an unimportant position within society; to make powerless

Minstrel (n)

White men who performed in Blackface while supporting negative stereotypes

Racism (n)

belief that there are natural differences between people who are different colors and that one race is superior to others

Recession (n)

a period of a downward turn in business (sales, profits)

Recidivism (n)
the tendency of a convicted criminal to commit additional crimes

Respectability Politics (adj.)
attempts by members within marginalized groups to police the behavior, appearance, and attitudes of other members by maintaining that they should behave in a way that is more acceptable to the mainstream group in order to prevent acts of violence

Segregation (n)
the enforced separation of different racial groups

Slave Trade (n)
the business of procuring and trading human beings for slavery and profit

Slavery (n)
the keeping of slaves as a practice (i.e. holding others in bondage)

Stigmatize (v)
to mark with shame

Subjugation (n)
the act or process of bringing one under control, enslavement

Suffrage (n)
the right to vote

Systemic Racism (n)
racism whose practice is embedded into legal and social policies

• •

Answers
for Comprehension

Section 1

1. A, C, B
2. B, D
3. C
4. A, D

5. T
6. F
7. F
8. T

9. desegregate
10. Ruby Bridges
11. superior
12. minstrel

Section 2

1. A
2. C
3. A, D
4. C

5. F
6. F
7. T
8. T

9. Roper v. Simmons
10. extremists
11. Post-Traumatic Stress Disorder or depression
12. Tarana Burke

Essay & Discussion Questions

The Short Answer Questions and Overall Essay Questions are subjective. Sharing your answers with teachers and family can be a positive way to spark conversations in your community.

About the Author

Kristina Brooke Daniele (pronounced Dan-YELL-ee) is a homeschooling mom, education consultant, former classroom teacher, freelance writer, and serial entrepreneur. As an English teacher at Harry S. Truman High School in The Bronx, New York, Kristina worked to increase the literacy skills of high schoolers who were often ignored by the system. Rather than rote memorization, Kristina engaged them in discussions of the real world and worlds within literature, preferring to aim for a holistic approach rather than focusing exclusively on their test scores. Her experience in the classroom informed her decision to homeschool her daughter. Both motivate her to continue to produce material that centers Black people within American history rather than as a footnote.

Kristina resides in Arizona with her husband and daughter. When she is not working her dream job, her nose is in a book or she is enjoying time with her family and close friends.

Connect with her at:
facebook.com/kristinabrookedaniele/

About the Illustrator

Lindsey Bailey is an artist and illustrator based in Memphis, TN. A BFA in Graphic Design from Mississippi State University morphed into a love for illustration. Known online under the moniker "LindseySwop", she has worked on character design, children's books, book covers and web graphics. A wife and mother, in her spare time she enjoys comics, pop culture, and movies. She draws inspiration from fashion, sci fi, and fantasy. Her works place POC, specifically women, into mundane settings with a twist of the unknown.

Connect with her at:
facebook.com/lindseyswop

Recommended Reading

Anderson, Laurie Halse. *Ashes*. Atheneum Books for Young Readers, 2016.

Anderson, Laurie Halse. *Chains*. Atheneum Children'S Books, 2016.

Anderson, Laurie Halse. *Forge*. Thorndike Press, 2017.

Asim, Jabari, and Bryan Collier. *Fifty Cents and a Dream: Young Booker T. Washington*. Little, Brown and Co., 2012.

Bridges, Ruby. *Ruby Bridges Goes to School: My True Story*. Scholastic Inc, 2010.

Clark-Robinson, Monica, and Frank Morrison. *Let the Children March*. Houghton Mifflin Harcourt, 2018.

Curtis, Christopher Paul. *The Watsons Go to Birmingham--1963*. Thorndike Press, a Part of Gale, Cengage Learning, 2017.

Daniele, Kristina Brooke. "10 Black Women Pioneers to Know for Black History Month." *Woo! Jr. Kids Activities*, 14 Feb. 2018, www.woojr.com/10-Black-women-pioneers-to-know-for-Black-history-month/.

Daniele, Kristina Brooke. "Black Heroes of the American Revolution Activities and Lesson Plan." *Woo! Jr. Kids Activities*, Woo! Jr. Kids Activities, 12 Oct. 2017, www.woojr.com/Black-heroes-american-revolution-activities-lesson-plan/.

Davis, Burke. *Black Heroes of the American Revolution*. Harcourt, 2007.

Evans, Shane. *We March*. Square Fish, 2016.

Feldman, Thea, and Alyssa Petersen. *Katherine Johnson*. Simon Spotlight, 2017.

Giovanni, Nikki, and Bryan Collier. *Rosa*. Zaner-Bloser, 2013.

Haber, Louis. *Black Pioneers of Science and Invention*. Odyssey Classic/Harcourt, 1992.

Haskins, James, and Benny Andrews. *Delivering Justice: W.W. Law and the Fight for Civil Rights*. Candlewick Press, 2006.

Hoose, Phillip M. *Claudette Colvin: Twice toward Justice*. Farrar Straus Giroux, 2014.

Jazynka, Kitson. *George Washington Carver*. National Geographic, 2016.

Levinson, Cynthia, and Vanessa Brantley-Newton. *The Youngest Marcher: the Story of Audrey Faye Hendricks, a Young Civil Rights Activist*. Atheneum Books for Young Readers, an Imprint of Simon & Schuster Children's Pub. Division, 2017.

Lewis, J. Patrick, and Jim Burke. *When Thunder Comes Poems for Civil Rights Leaders*. Chronicle Books, 2013.

Magoon, Kekla. *The Rock and the River*. Simon & Schuster Children's Pub., 2010.

McKinstry, Carolyn Maull, and Denise George. *While the World Watched: a Birmingham Bombing Survivor Comes of Age during the Civil Rights Movement*. Tyndale House Publishers, 2011.

Meyers, Walter Dean. *Malcolm X A Fire Burning Brightly*. Paw Prints, 2009.

Myers, Walter Dean. *Ida b. Wells: Let the Truth Be Told*. Amistad, 2015.

Powell, Patricia Hruby, and Shadra Strickland. *Loving vs. Virginia: a Documentary Novel of the Landmark Civil Rights Case*. Chronicle Books, 2017.

Rochelle, Belinda. *Witnesses to Freedom: Young People Who Fought for Civil Rights*. Puffin, 1997.

Sanders, Nancy I. *America's Black Founders: Revolutionary Heroes and Early Leaders: with 21 Activities*. Chicago Review Press, 2010.

Scattergood, Augusta. *Glory Be*. Scholastic Press, 2012.

Shelton, Paula Young, and Raul Colon. *Child of the Civil Rights Movement*. Schwartz & Wade Books, 2010.

Shetterly, Margot Lee, et al. *Hidden Figures: the True Story of Four Black Women and the Space Race*. HarperCollins Children's Books, 2018.

Stefoff, Rebecca, and Howard Zinn. *A Young People's History of the United States: Columbus to the War on Terror*. Seven Stories Press, 2009.

References

2013 Anti-Islam Legislation. (2017, October 12). Retrieved from http://www.islamophobia.org/articles/137-2013-anti-islam-legislation.html

About. (n.d.). Retrieved from http://occupywallst.org/about/
Altbach, P. G. (1966). "Black Power" and the US Civil Rights Movement. 1(6), 233-234. Retrieved April 24, 2018, from http://www.jstor.org/stable/4356980

Baum, D. (1997). *Smoke and mirrors: The war on drugs and the politics of failure*. Boston: Back Bay Books.

Birchett, C., Boyd, T., Carruthers, I. E., Johnson, A. G., & Alexander, M. (2011). *The new Jim Crow: Mass incarceration in the age of colorblindness*. Chicago, IL: Samuel DeWitt Proctor Conference.

Bobo, L. D., Johnson, D., Warren, P. Y., & Farrell, A. (2015). *Trayvon Martin, Race, and the Criminal Justice System*. NYU Press. Retrieved April 24, 2018, from http://www.jstor.org/stable/j.ctt15zc702

Bowen, D. (2016, January 16). 4 ways the War on Drugs disproportionately affects the world's poor. Retrieved from https://www.globalcitizen.org/en/content/4-ways-the-war-on-drugs-disproportionately-affects/

Clarkson, T. (n.d.). The History of the Rise, Progress and Accomplishment of the Abolition of the African Slave Trade by the British Parliament (1808)Volume II by Clarkson, Thomas, 1760-1846. Retrieved from https://www.scribd.com/document/2375417/The-History-of-the-Rise-Progress-and-Accomplishment-of-the-Abolition-of-the-African-Slave-Trade-by-the-British-Parliament-1808-Volume-II-by-Clarkson

Cleaver, E. (1999). *Soul on ice*. New York, NY: Delta Trade Paperbacks.

Coles, R., & Ford, G. (2012). *The story of Ruby Bridges*. Toronto: CNIB.

Davis, B. (2007). *Black heroes of the American Revolution*. Orlando: Harcourt.

DuVernay, A. (Director). (2016). *13th* [Video file]. United States: Netflix. Retrieved from https://www.netflix.com/title/80091741.

Flatlow, N. (2014, September 11). What Has Changed About Police Brutality In America, From Rodney King To Michael Brown. Retrieved from https://thinkprogress.org/what-has-changed-about-police-brutality-in-america-from-rodney-king-to-michael-brown-e6b29a2feff8/

Fulton, S. (2017). *Rest in Power: The Enduring Life of Trayvon Martin*. Spiegel & Grau.

Garza, A., Cullors, P., & Tometi, O. (n.d.). Herstory. Retrieved from https://Blacklivesmatter.com/about/herstory/

Giovanni, N., & Collier, B. (2013). *Rosa*. Columbus, O.H.: Zaner-Bloser.

Goldenburg, D. M. (2016). *The Curse of Ham Race and Slavery in Early Judaism, Christianity, and Islam*. Paw Prints.

The Great Recession. (n.d.). Retrieved from http://stateofworkingamerica.org/great-recession/

Heroes. (n.d.). Retrieved from http://www.freedomcenter.org/enabling-freedom/heroes

Hills, D. D., & Curry, T. J. (2015). State Violence, Black Bodies, and Martin Luther King's Black Power. 3(4), 453-469. doi:10.5325/jafrireli.3.4.0453

History.com Staff. (2009). Civil Rights Movement. Retrieved from https://www.history.com/topics/Black-history/civil-rights-movement

History.com Staff. (2017). Great Recession. Retrieved from https://www.history.com/topics/recession

Important Supreme Court Cases for Civil Rights. (n.d.). Retrieved from https://civilrights.org/judiciary/federal-court-system/important-supreme-court-cases-civil-rights/

Islamophobia 101. (2017, September 29). Retrieved from http://www.islamophobia.org/research/islamophobia-101.html

Islamophobia and its impact in the United States: Same hate new target [PDF]. (2010, December). Council on American-Islamic Relations.

Islamophobia in the 2014 Elections. (2017, October 12). Retrieved from http://www.islamophobia.org/articles/156-islamophobia-in-the-2014-elections.html

Islamphobia and its impact in the United States: Legislating fear [PDF]. (2012, December). Council on American-Islamic Relations.

Kain, E. (2011, October 27). The War on Drugs is a War on Minorities and the Poor. Retrieved from https://www.forbes.com/sites/erikkain/2011/06/28/the-war-on-drugs-is-a-war-on-minorities-and-the-poor/#351b7255624c

Kelly, K. C. (2016, April 28). Defense of Marriage Act. Retrieved from https://www.britannica.com/topic/Defense-of-Marriage-Act

King, M. L., Jr. (1963, April 16). Letter From a Birmingham Jail. Retrieved from https://kinginstitute.stanford.edu/king-papers/documents/letter-birmingham-jail

L. (2015, April 16). These maps show the war on drugs is mostly fought in poor neighborhoods. Retrieved from https://www.vox.com/2015/4/16/8431283/drug-war-poverty

Lee, C. (2013). Making Race Salient: Trayvon Martin and Implicit Bias in a Not Yet Post-Racial Society. Retrieved from https://scholarship.law.gwu.edu/faculty_publications/728/

Lee, S. (Director). (2001). *A Huey P. Newton story* [Motion picture on DVD].

Levine, E. S. (2008). *Freedom's Children Young Civil Rights Activists Tell Their Own Stories*. Paw Prints.

Lugo-Lugo, C. R., & Bloodsworth-Lugo, M. K. (2009). Black as Brown: The 2008 Obama Primary Campaign and the U.S. Browning of Terror. *13*(2), 110-120. Retrieved April 24, 2018, from http://www.jstor.org/stable/41819197

Marable, M. (2012). *Malcolm X: A Life of Reinvention*. New York: Guilford Publication.

McSpadden, L., & LeFlore, L. B. (2016). *Tell the truth & shame the devil: The life, legacy, and love of my son Michael Brown*. New York: Regan Arts.

Olson, L. (2002). *Freedom's daughters: The unsung heroines of the Civil Rights Movement from 1830 to 1970*. New York: Simon & Schuster.

Parham-Payne, W. V. (2009). Through the Lens of Black Women: The Significance of Obama's Campaign. *13*(2), 131-138. Retrieved April 24, 2018, from http://www.jstor.org/stable/41819199

Ralph, L., & Chance, K. (2014). Legacies of Fear. (113), 137-143. doi:10.2979/transition.113.137

Rethink the War on Drugs. (n.d.). Retrieved from https://www.healthpovertyaction.org/speaking-out/rethink-the-war-on-drugs/

Robinson, J. A. (1987). *Montgomery Bus Boycott*. Tenn: Univ. of Tenn.

Saul, E. (Ed.). (n.d.). Abolitionists and Anti-Slavery Activists. Retrieved from http://www.americanabolitionists.com/abolitionists-and-anti-slavery-activists.html

Social Security. (n.d.). Retrieved from https://www.ssa.gov/history/tally1996.html

Staff, I. (2018, April 07). Dodd-Frank Wall Street Reform and Consumer Protection Act. Retrieved from https://www.investopedia.com/terms/d/dodd-frank-financial-regulatory-reform-bill.asp

The USA PATRIOT Act: Preserving Life and Liberty. (n.d.). Retrieved from https://www.justice.gov/archive/ll/highlights.htm

What we believe. (n.d.). Retrieved from https://Blacklivesmatter.com/about/what-we-believe/

Williams, J. (1987). *Eyes on the prize: America's civil rights years, 1954-1965*. New York, NY: Viking.

Women's Political Council (WPC) of Montgomery. (1949, March 01). Retrieved from https://kinginstitute.stanford.edu/encyclopedia/womens-political-council-wpc-montgomery

Yanow, D. (2016, May 17). Evidence-based policy. Retrieved from https://www.britannica.com/topic/evidence-based-policy#ref1181135

Zinn, H. (2008). *A people's history of the United States: 1492 - present*. New York, NY: HarperCollins.

Photograph Credits

Page 2
Engraving by W. Roberts of the Emancipation Proclamation
United States Library of Congress
https://en.wikipedia.org/wiki/Emancipation_Proclamation#/
media/File:Emancipation_Proclamation.jpg

Page 9
Photograph of the Civil Rights March on Washington
Scherman, Rowland, Photographer
https://catalog.archives.gov/id/542044

Page 11
Little Rock Nine
New York World-Telegram and the Sun staff photographer:
Albertin, Walter, photographer
https://commons.wikimedia.org/wiki/File:Robert_F._Wagner_
with_Little_Rock_students_NYWTS.jpg

Page 13
1960 Sit In
State Archives of North Carolina
https://www.flickr.com/photos/north-carolina-state-
archives/24495308926/

Page 14
Ella Baker
The Ella Baker Center for Human Rights
https://upload.wikimedia.org/wikipedia/commons/0/02/
EllaBaker.jpg

Page 16
Founding Members of the Black Panther Party
https://en.wikipedia.org/wiki/File:Black-Panther-Party-
founders-newton-seale-forte-howard-hutton.jpg

Page 20
Warren Court
United States Library of Congress
https://en.wikipedia.org/wiki/Brown_v._Board_of_Education#/
media/File:Warren_Court_1953.jpg

Page 28
Ronald Reagan signing Japanese reparations bill
Ronald Reagan Presidential library
https://en.wikipedia.org/wiki/Civil_Liberties_Act_of_1988#/
media/File:Ronald_Reagan_signing_Japanese_reparations_bill.
jpg

Page 29
Bill Clinton signing bill
Staff Sgt. Scott M. Ash, U.S. Air Force
https://commons.wikimedia.org/wiki/File:Defense.gov_News_
Photo_991005-F-2270A-003.jpg

Page 36
Occupy Wall Street Protest
Michael Fleshman
https://www.flickr.com/photos/fleshmanpix/6840363064/

Page 50
Emanuel African Methodist Episcopal Church
Cal Sr
https://commons.wikimedia.org/wiki/File:Emanuel_African_
Methodist_Episcopal_(AME)_Church_Corrected.jpg

Page 51
No Justice No Peace protest sign
Mark Dixon
https://flic.kr/p/q2qxAN

Page 52
Black Lives Matter protest
Johnny Silvercloud
https://flic.kr/p/KooLg9

Made in the USA
Monee, IL
03 June 2020